DISTANCIAS / DISTANCES

For cousins Marine &
Ralph with love

Renata

Tulsa OK
January 1994

Susana Thénon

➤   ➤   ➤

distancias / distances

➤   ➤   ➤

Translated with an Introduction and
Afterword by Renata Treitel
With an Epilogue by Ana María Barrenechea

SUN &
MOON

CLASSICS

40

LOS ANGELES
SUN & MOON PRESS
1994

Sun & Moon Press
A Program of The Contemporary Arts Educational Project, Inc.
a nonprofit corporation
6026 Wilshire Boulevard, Los Angeles, California 90036

This edition first published in paperback in 1994 by Sun & Moon Press
10 9 8 7 6 5 4 3 2 1
FIRST EDITION
© Torres Agüero Editor, 1984
Translation © Renata Treitel, 1994
Reprinted by permission
Biographical information © Sun & Moon Press, 1994
All rights reserved

Some of these poems have previously appeared in *Caliban, Helicon Nine,
Latin American Literary Review, Mundus Artium, New Orleans Review, Nimrod,
Raddle Moon,* and *Rohwedder.* The translator wishes to thank
the editors of these magazines.

This book was made possible, in part, through an operational grant from the
Andrew W. Mellon Foundation and through contributions to
The Contemporary Arts Educational Project, Inc.,
a nonprofit corporation

Cover: photograph by Susana Thénon
Design: Katie Messborn

LIBRARY OF CONGRESS CATALOGING IN PUBLICATION DATA
Thénon, Susana [1937–1990]
distancias/distances
p. cm – (Sun & Moon Classics: 40)
ISBN: 1-55713-153-8
I. Title. II. Series.
811'.54–dc20

Printed in the United States of America on acid-free paper.

My deepest and fondest thanks go to those who supported the making of this book. To Ana María Barrenechea who, without dismay, encouraged me critically for many difficult years; to Renata Treitel who, by her own initiative, translated these poems into English, skillfully clearing away all sorts of difficulties.

And special thanks go to Iris Scaccheri whose dancing, unbeknownst to her, inspired the definite vision I needed to revise and complete this work which was threatening to become interminable.

S. T.

Contents

➢   ➢   ➢

➢   ➢   ➢

Foreword

I am grateful to Ana Rosa Genijovich who introduced me to Susana Thénon in Buenos Aires, Argentina, in 1978. I am also grateful to Susana Thénon herself who generously helped me with the growing number of problems of interpretation. Her help was given by correspondence mainly during 1982 and early 1983 and again personally when we met in Buenos Aires in October 1983.

Ana María Barrenechea helped me on problems of interpretation of the whole work, both during her stay at Columbia University in the springs 1982 and 1983, and again in October 1984 in Buenos Aires, when she graciously accepted to be interviewed together with Susana Thénon on the subject of *distancias*.

On this side of the hemisphere, I am grateful to Charles Kenmitz who first collaborated with me on five poems from the book. One of the poems (now number 3) appeared in slightly different form in *The New Orleans Review*, to whose editors I feel indebted for being the first in the United States to recognize the poetical gift of Ms. Thénon. For problems in English, Diane Glancy and Ann Zoller–poets in their own right–read the manuscript carefully with me. Their insights brought me closer to the original and spurred me in a meticulous search for the *mot juste* in English.

Elizabeth Gamble Miller, of Southern Methodist University, American translator of Hugo Lindo's poetry, did a critical reading of my translation. I am also indebted to Ms. Miller for giving me the opportunity to present some of the problems I encountered in translating Thénon at the Spanish Workshop during the 1983 American Literary Translators Association (ALTA) Conference in New Orleans.

Finally, my thanks are also due to my family: my husband for being, in more ways than one, my Buenos Aires connection; my daughter Corinna for participating in the many philosophical and metaphysical issues raised by *distancias*; my sons Geoffrey and Michael for help in collating the manuscript; and my daughter Nadine for being herself.

Introduction

Well-versed in the classics, translator from the ancient Greek, translator of Rilke, artistic photographer, poet–Susana Thénon belongs to what, in the 1969 issue of *Mundus Artium*, Ramón Xirau called "The New Generation," the group of post-World War II Latin American poets, born between 1924 and 1940, whose work was in full process of development at the time Mr. Xirau was writing.

Xirau divides "The New Generation" poets into two groupings, "poets of protest," citing among others the names of Ernesto Cardenal (Nicaragua) and Enrique Lihn (Chile), and "poets with a lyric tendency," such as Blanca Varela (Peru), Rosario Castellanos (Mexico), Jaime Sabines (Mexico), Marco Antonio Montes de Oca (Mexico), Alejandra Pizarnik (Argentina), José Emilio Pacheco (Mexico) and others.

Chronologically Susana Thénon belongs to "The New Generation." However, she is an innovator, and her work has great affinity with writers outside her country. Her early poetic work, *Edad sin tregua* (1958), *Habitante de la nada* (1960), *de lugares extraños* (1967), displays Biblical and classical roots. Her style is terse and combines clarity of vision with economy of means. By contrast, *distancias* (1984) marks a turning point, and Susana Thénon herself is first in admitting the change. "If you find them difficult," she wrote to me about *distancias* in February 1979, "it is because they *are* difficult." When I pressed questions concerning the sudden obscurity of her work, she replied, "I don't know how it was that I began to write this way. I only know that it happened. And I too was very surprised. Afterwards, I realized that without quite knowing how, I had entered a strange zone from which it would be difficult to return."

Like most writers of her generation, Thénon is influenced by the romantic aesthetics, by surrealism, existentialism, anthropology, linguistics, psychoanalysis. But she also recognizes her indebtedness to the Italian writers of the 1960s, the so-called *I Novissimi*, a group of avant-garde writers with whom she shares matters of form, lack of traditional syntax, violence of language and images,

[10]

fragmentation. Like them, she breaks the traditional relationship of reader and writer and, intentionally, engages the reader in the very process of creation. "The reader is an active being who participates in the act of creation," she wrote to me in 1979; "...genders, numbers, plurals, agreements are obstacles and therefore I skip them (but only when it is necessary: I do not want to substitute one rhetoric for another nor establish a code.") She also recognizes her indebtedness to American poets: T. S. Eliot and, especially, e.e. cummings, many of whose typographical devices have found a way into *distancias* (i.e., poems number 8, 24, 29, 31, and others). "I *love*," she wrote to me in 1979, "T.S. Eliot and e.e. cummings among others whose names I may eventually remember." And then, at my request, she sent an approximate list of her readings in poetry. Among the Italians: Eugenio Montale, Salvatore Quasimodo, Alfonso Gatto, Cesare Pavese, Vittorio Sereni and Bruno Nardini; among the Brazilians: C. Drummond de Andrade, from whom she borrows the epigraph to *distancias*, Augusto Frederico Schmidt, and Manuel Bandeira; the Germans: Novalis, Hölderlin, George, Rilke, and at the moment she was writing, Helmut Heissenbüttel and Hans Magnus Enzensberger; the Spanish: Federico García Lorca and Vicente Aleixandre (and lots of Góngora and Fray Luis de León). She admits having no ties to speak of with the French or the Surrealists. Then, almost as an afterthought, she mentions the Greek and Roman writers.

distancias, a collection of 39 poems, was written between 1967 and 1982. It was not published until 1984. Its striking feature is form, a circle: the first poem is also the last one, so that a dialectic between structure and the opening lines is established at the very beginning. If "forms have meanings," as Octavio Paz has suggested, the reader of *distancias* must be willing to enter its form and let it "secrete its ideas, its vision of the world" because, again Octavio Paz's voice, the problem of poetry's meaning "...is not what the words say, but what is said between them."

For the present translator, the task has been very rewarding in spite of the many difficulties, among which I would like to mention three: an original manuscript that was truly in the making while the translation was under way, total lack of critical material, and an almost total lack of a comparable poetic tradition in English.

distancias is a pioneer's work. Despite inevitable similarities with writers of our times, Thénon is an authentic voice and her work is unique.

Latin American poetry in the 20th Century has a splendid tradition and many American poets are looking to their Latin American counterparts for renewal. To borrow again from Ramón Xirau and, indirectly, from Octavio Paz, Susana Thénon's poetry is *"poesía en movimiento"* in the double sense of the meaning: it belongs to a body of work that is in full growth and it is also poetry in process, in constant metamorphosis, so that the pitch of her poetic experience reaches the reader as sheer radiance:

> #1
> ...   face to the sky it is not possible
> that she should still burn more should burn still more
> burn alone eternal as if the wind   ...

or

> #12
>
> the embrace the embrace in the afternoon
> how immortal i have been
> and how little the alien future hurts
> this stone without rest   you were eternal still
> you were the last the first the nothing
> and nothing but   sun   your glance my blindness
> sun forever yesterday   and we turned night
> and the embrace was the sea

More than once, as I was translating *distancias*, Heidegger's words about Hölderlin would come to mind. To this day, when I think of Susana Thénon and her work, I cannot but feel I am in the presence of a "poets' poet."

−Renata Treitel
January 1984

a S.C.

Observa:
yermas de melodía y de concepto,
las palabras se refugian en la noche.
Aun húmedas e impregnadas de sueño
ruedan en un río difícil y se transforman en desprecio.

Carlos Drummond de Andrade
Procura de la poesía

To   S.C.

Watch:
barren of melody and meaning,
the words seek refuge in the night.
Still damp and pregnant with sleep
they roll in a difficult river and turn into contempt

Carlos Drummond de Andrade
In Search of Poetry

la rueda se ha detenido   se ha deteni-
dos tres dos tres dos   la rueda
se ha detenido   roto por dentro
solo madera   entran ojos
solo memoria   cónico
solo memoria   al cielo de cara no es posible
que arda ya más que arda más todavía   que
arda sola eterna como si el viento   (algo)
no arrojara sus migas sus ropas   deshecho
ansiado cuerpo luz de la noche   pájaros
homicidas bajo el puente   se alejan fríos
(algo) cadenciosos   mar
y silbó y dijo   criatura barro
y dijo y rió   trompa de vena
y rió apuntó   carne temblada
y disparó   bulto
              zapatos
              carne
aéreo   (algo)
y sol   (una mujer)
hachas de sol   (ante la puerta con llave)
arañan la puerta   (busca su llave) aclara

the wheel has stopped   stop–
two three two three two   the wheel
has stopped   broken inside
only wood   eyes enter
only memory   conic
only memory   face to the sky it is not possible
that she should still burn more should burn still more
burn alone eternal as if the wind   (something)
would not scatter her crumbs her clothes   undone
desired body light of the night   birds
homicides under the bridge   go away cold
(something) in cadence   sea
and it whistled and said   creature mud
said and laughed   trumpet of vein
laughed aimed   trembled flesh
and fired   bundle
            shoes
            flesh
ethereal   (something)
and sun   (a woman)
hatchets of sun   (before the locked door)
scratch the door   (looks for her key) it clears

el pecho (dice en alta voz) el ojo (ábreme yo) la
                                        [mano
(llama llama) el borde (no) del río (no) de sangre
(no) de sangre que huye hilo salvaje negro de pavor
entre el suelo y la puerta al encuentro de sus pasos
la rueda se ha detenido   se ha deteni–
dos tres dos tres dos   la rueda
se ha detenido

her chest (says in a loud voice) her eye (open to me i) her
                                                    [hand
(calls calls) the edge (no) of the river (no) of blood
(no) of blood that runs away wild thread black with fear
between threshold and door meeting her steps
the wheel has stopped   stop-
two three two three two   the wheel
has stopped

de cara a la pared
dibujan los ojos dan movimiento
amor y el salto al otro lado
es otro hueco   y toda la presencia
otra pared límite blando familiar
la mirada una casa para siempre
solas mesas tendidas
el mundo un paso y otro paso   otro paso

un canal donde atascarse con algunos cuchillos con algunos
reinos negros con algunas novedades del silencio y del sol

➤   2

facing the wall
the eyes draw give motion
love and the jump the other side
is another hollow   and all the presence
another wall boundary soft and familiar
the glance a house forever
tables set alone
the world one step another step   other step

a canal where to get trapped with some knives with some
black kingdoms with some news about the silence and the sun

➤   3

ahora se abate la locura del poema
sobre la calle en ruinas   donde fuimos
somos qué   bajo cifra mortal
aunque lloremos   por la boca por la mano
lágrima tan usada invisible
y en las ollas comunes
murmure el pan   su tétano sus ángeles

➤   3

now the madness of the poem swoops
on the street in ruins   where we were
what are   under mortal cipher
even if we cry   through the mouth through the hand
tear so worn out invisible
and in the common pots
bread murmurs   its tetanus its angels

➤　　4

hay un país　　(pero no el mío)
donde la noche es solo por la tarde
(pero no el nuestro)
y así canta una estrella su tiempo libre

toda la muerte pensaré
ya que morir no es mío
y aún alumbro con sangre deslumbrada
(hay un país) *el sueño de caída*
(hay un país)
y yo conmigo (y siempre)
de amor inmóviles

➤ 4

there's a country   (but not mine)
where night is only in the afternoon
(but not ours)
and thus sings a star its free time

throughout death i will think
since dying is not mine
and I still shine with dazzled blood
(there's a country) *the dream of falling*
(there's a country)
and i with myself (and always)
with love unmoved

➤   5

el rayo en la cabeza
de oro nacido   para jugar
desembocada–
mente al pájaro mental

oh moira
OH MOIRA
carne de viento en la mirada
oh tú alegría
de fingir muerte a lo que amas

bello animal desgracia
posado en lo indecible

➤   5

ray in the head
born of gold   to play
inordinate–
ly mental bird

o moira
O MOIRA
flesh of wind in the glance
o you joy
of feigning death to what you love

beautiful animal–misfortune
perched on the unutterable

la gran serpiente abrazada al mundo
duerme   también tú duermes
yo duermo   puros de sonido
sonreímos contra la   desesperada y sola
entre las flores   no
(puedes) no (no puedes)   y del día
llueve sombra   amanecida tiemblas de
muerte   anterior a la muerte
duermo extraña al mapa de los mares   aquí leo
tu sueño   aquí ya no   leo
tu risa lobo idioma blanco   yo descifro
no (no puedes no)
y ahora
cae la gota (bebe amor)
con todo un cielo de apretada locura

the great snake that embraces the world
sleeps   you too sleep
i sleep   pure of sound
we smile against the   desperate and alone
among the flowers   no
(you can) no (you cannot)   and of the day
it rains shadow   dawned you tremble with
death   prior to death
i sleep a stranger to the map of the seas   here i read
your dream   no longer here   i read
your wolf–laughter white language   i decipher
no (you cannot no)
and now
the drop falls (drink love)
with a whole sky of packed madness

tu paso   nunca otro   *y tu boca*
roída por el viento   criatura
individual   en un mundo de nombres
que ya apenas pronuncias   y que apenas te hieren
dulce materia   viva
en tierra enferma   *criatura*
individual   entre flor y flor oscura
tu paso   nunca otro
y tu boca roída por el viento

your step   never another   *and your mouth*
gnawed by the wind   individual
creature   in a world of names
you now barely utter   that barely wound you
gentle stuff   alive
on sick earth   *individual*
creature   between flower and flower dark
your step   never another
and your mouth gnawed by the wind

al sueño mayor
donde vuelven a hablarse el espanto y la música
vidas lo aman de abajo
en corrupción benigna   dueño
de oros vencidos (pero) en
quiniela oscura que algo can( )ta

➤   8

the main dream
where terror and music talk to each other again
life loves it from below
in benign corruption   master
of defeated golds (but) in
dark lottery that sing( )s something

cavidad   tú
lo otro   llama
amor   congrega
dos una vez   una sola vez
preciencia cuando abraza   abierto
cúpula   estoy
veníamos de atrás   verano
ignorantes   sin compuerta
el viento hidraba (flujos) acuérdate
de sol   velarios me impiden
cuando se borre   sí
    nuestra mordida paralaje
y nos disuelva sin rumor y nos separe el día

hollow   you
the other   calls
love   assembles
two once   once only
prescience when it embraces   open
dome   i am
we came from before   summer
ignorant   without flood-gate
the hydra-wind was howling (fluxes) remember
sun   veils hinder me
when *our bitten parallax*   yes
     fades away
and the day dissolves us without noise and keeps us apart

con el martirio
(picadura infinita)
con el violín
de lata crapulosa

con el martirio
al hombro
porque sí porque sí
(nunca por ¿ah?
por ¿ih?)

con el martirio

el rojo oficio errante
de extinguirse

➢ 10

with martyrdom
(infinite sting)
with the violin
of debauched tinsel

with martyrdom
on the shoulder
because because
(never for ah?
for auh?)

with martyrdom

the red roving art
of dying out

ave naranjas una sierra de sol
roe mis ojos noche en dos
miles de nada (a mi alcance)
pero un trago de risa
ya no barre con el miedo come luz
y gira en su luna que es inmortal
y nunca y sin remedio la última

bird oranges a saw of sun
gnaws my eyes night into two
thousands of nothing (at my reach)
but a draft of laughter
no longer sweeps away the fear eats light
and turns on its moon which is immortal
and never and hopelessly the last

edipo

el abrazo el abrazo en la tarde
qué inmortal he sido
y qué poco lastima el porvenir extranjero
esta piedra sin descanso   eras eterna todavía
eras lo último y primero y nada
y nada sino   sol   tu mirada mi ceguera
sol para siempre ayer   y anochecimos
y el abrazo era el mar

œdipus

the embrace the embrace in the afternoon
how immortal i have been
and how little the alien future hurts
this stone without rest   you were eternal still
you were the last the first the nothing
and nothing but   sun   your glance my blindness
sun forever yesterday   and we turned night
and the embrace was the sea

la noche

amparo desamparada
amparo nictálope
delicada combustible
amparo esta vieja cáscara
entre tantas otras
que revienta de fuegos olorosos
pólvora niña
y razón pura vertebrados eximios

y el ojo crece
desaloja dispara manos
y el ojo súbitamente carne
va al encuentro de lo ciego
destila en bares no llanto pero sí
hierro escualos sopa venérea
y el ojo de ciudad repentina
se pierde en el museo de la cólera

the night

i shelter unsheltered
i shelter day blind
delicate flammable
i shelter this old shell
among so many other shells
that bursts with stinking fires
child–gunpowder
and pure reason exalted vertebrates

and the eye grows
ejects fires the hands
and the eye suddenly flesh
goes to meet the unseeing
distills in bars not tears but
iron sharks venereal soup
and the eye of sudden city
gets lost in the museum of wrath

cuerpo sin funeral
rueda el hijo como una luna

como otra vez
en mi espanto lleno de crujidos
en mi valija de ave
la muchacha infutura
bebe su nombre idiota

mi leve lengua
empollo
sobre esta grieta
cómplice amarga
del despertar sin día
me alimento de párpado brillo de alondra muerta

body without funeral
the son rolls like a moon

like that other time
in my creak–filled horror
in my suitcase of bird
the futureless girl
drinks her foolish name

i brood
my light tongue
on this crack
bitter accomplice
of the dayless awakening
i feed on eyelid shine of dead lark

la belleza en su costumbre
chista al que pasa entre dientes de botella
sopla casi dormido   jardín
que nadie ve   nadie sembró

las iglesias   larga sangre
decrecen con la lluvia
turbia de mujeres   de monos
de osamentas como casas   de flores

beauty by habit
whistles at the one who goes through bottle teeth
there blows almost asleep   garden
that no one perceives   no one seeded

churches   long blood
dwindle with the rain
murky with women   with monkeys
with skeletons like houses   with flowers

no quedaban tabernas hubo entonces que dormirse
loco a secas limpiamente violín
y hermano memorioso de David Bach
y como él inexistente de sol a sol
sin dar el paso a qué (pero sin duda oscuro)
cementerios de nieve igual
a noches

➢ 15

no bars left so one had to sleep
crazy dry cleanly violin
and memoried brother of David Bach
and like him inexistent from sun to sun
without taking the step to whatever (dark no doubt)
cemeteries of snow just like
nights

anunciación

imagen vi veo
bebo con santa o satán y
antiguo *landscape* orificio a Gante
donde posó una virgen algo estrábica
para su donante banquero famoso
por su
devoción y obras

pías

annunciation

image i saw see
i drink with saint or satan and
ancient *Landschaft* opening on Ghent
where a slightly cross–eyed virgin sat
for her famous banker–donor
for his
devotion and

charities

cuánto demora el tiempo
(bosques aquellos)
dolor doler   que no deja
(bosques a viento)

habla la noche en lengua muerta

soy dos
una igual una
sin siempre

➢ 17

how long time takes
(those woods)
grief to grieve   that does not let
(wind woods)

the night speaks a dead language

i am two
one equal one
without forever

desvélate
lube sobre agua
gota mar   lejos los días
querer   lejos la espalda
lastimado   querer (tus
árbol caballería de copas)
    volar oar volar
levan el aire   sorprendían
    pájaros del regreso
cada fuego salino ayer

keep watch
cloon* on water
drop sea   far the days
to love   far the shoulder
hurt   to love (your
tree cavalry of cups)
    to fly igh to fly
    homing birds
lift air   would surprise
each salt–fire yesterday

* *cloon: combination of first two letters of "cloud" and last three of "moon". This is in keeping with the original though in reverse order.*

luna como antigua música
que alguien sorprende viva
en los jardines del Club Social
a esas horas que no cuentan
(rió él   es decir   yo)
de una vida

➤   19

moon like ancient music
one catches alive
in the gardens of the Social Club
at those hours that do not count
(he laughed   that is   i)
in one's life

edipo

otra vez a pesar de las nubes
ciegas (me quemaba) te amé di sangre
por tus flores   te llamé tierra
soplé coronas   hilo
de un tiempo en retroceso   morí
para nacer   te alzaban
mis hombros   sí temblor sueño carnívoro
fuiste la mañana   oí tus letras
suavemente en la habitación como pasos

œdipus

again despite the blind
clouds (i was burning) i loved you i bled
for your flowers   called you earth
blew wreaths   thread
of a time in regression   i died
to be born   my shoulders
were lifting you   yes shiver carnivorous sleep
you were the morning   i heard you spell
in the room soft like steps

sin luz el día el día
aquel día aquel gotera sin remedio sin
ay sin techo sin remedio sin cielo el
día aquel aquel   de hoy
miles de aquel
día de hoy   hijo de solo y sola
de la piedra   sola y solo de la piedra
el día aquel
de hoy

no light day day
that day that leak no hope no
ay no roof no hope no sky
day that one that one   of today
thousands of that
day of today   son of he–and–she alone
of the stone   she–and–he alone of the stone
day that
of today

respira en
el parque
lugar sobre sí mismo   dudosamente eterno y
(menos diez)   algo
en el parque

➢   22

    there breathes in
the park
place above itself   improbably eternal and
(ten to)   something
in the park

un ángel tísico guarda estas guerras
y nuestra desnudez aún banquete de sombras
preserva a todo tiempo de morir

solos noche de un siglo   vino de ojos
pira de abrahám   en casernas de olvido

por lo olvidado vuelven

➢   23

a consumptive angel guards these wars
and our nakedness still a banquet of shadows
preserves all time from dying

alone century-long night   wine of eyes
pyre of abraham   in barracks of forgetfulness

because forgotten they return

sin encuentro   lo imposible
(una mañana) seco
herido (y sus bengalas) edifica
un (y su flor) leve país
(de qué materia) un cielo agudo
contra el miedo frontero (lo imposible)
ya (y su flor

➢   24

without encounter   the impossible
(one morning) dry
wounded (and its fireworks) builds
a (and its flower) light country
(of what stuff) a sharp sky
against the impending fear (the impossible)
already (and its flower

no se dice   no
se dice   no decir
nada

esta noche   (nada)
la gangrena en el patio

➤   25

we don't say   no
we say   not to say
nothing

tonight   (nothing)
gangrene in the patio

sol menos uno sol
igual a sol

no entiendo

casa
el sombrero
piedra de afilar

no entiendo

otro buen día
y leche (sol) noticia
y bala cerco pan
noticia

qué   no entiendo
letra polo desagüe   simontemplar
caballo solución
rueda miseria cavidad (sol)
sol

sun minus one sun
equals sun

i don't understand

house
the hat
whetstone

i don't understand

another good day
and milk (sun) news
and bullet siege bread
news

what?   i don't understand
letter pole drain   spiderman
horse solution
wheel misery hollow (sun)
sun

desventaja
dictador vieja chiste
pregunta
pregunta
sala de estar mueca simposio
clan   abrigo sopa suerte
dictador

no entiendo   (*no entiende*)
no puedo   (*no puede*)
entender   (*no puede entender*)

no entiendo
soma hueso
carga
(sol) patio

sol
flor pastilla
navaja carta broche (dos)
cosa

perfil llave
amistad (sol) desván
juego
no entiendo
no

disadvantage
dictator hag joke
question
question
parlor grimace symposium
clan   coat soup luck
dictator

i don't understand   (*does not understand*)
i cannot   (*cannot*)
understand   (*cannot understand*)

i don't understand
soma bone
load
(sun) yard

sun
flower candy
razor letter clip (two)
thing

profile key
friendship (sun) garret
game
i don't understand
no

noticia
fila marca tablero dictador
cuerpo sonido
umbral invierno sangre
sol

SOL
menos uno sol
igual a sol

news
line notch board dictator
body sound
threshold winter blood
sun

SUN
minus one sun
equals sun

asesinato del espíritu santo

silencio de máuser

(avanza gallina sacra
estúpida coalición
de pluma)

pum   (eli eli)

murder of the holy ghost

silence of mauser

(come forward holy hen
stupid coalition of feather)

bang   (eli eli)

tarde   inglesa más bien
y juegos de palabras
para no oir que el ruiseñor repite *sangre sangre*
sobre todo si lunas de jardín
y julio bajo y denso
de rumor en galerías
tarde   inglesa más bien
donde el dueño del mundo
para no oir que el ruiseñor

afternoon   somewhat english
and word games
not to hear the nightingale repeat *blood blood*
above all if garden moons
and july low and dense
of whispers in galleries
afternoon   somewhat english
where the world master
not to hear the nightingale

y el odio
(y el drac
ma el dó
lar)

y el odio
(y siéntesespere
amor mío
en las muelas de mi sangre)

y el odio
(y sol menor
para cuerdas y continuo)

y el odio
(y asoma
el hijo de jíbaros
y es macrocéfalo)

y el odio
(y suba suba

and the hatred
(and the drac
hma the dol
lar)

and the hatred
(and sitandwait
my love
in the grindstones of my blood)

and the hatred
(and g minor
for strings and continuum)

and the hatred
(and there comes forth
the son of jivaros
and he is macrocephalic)

and the hatred
(and rise rise

Urizen
Ammón Râ)

y el
(Yog Sothoth)

y el
(odio ya hueso
médula ya)

(y el
odio)

oh fin
oh mariposa de mil años

Urizen
Amon–Ra)

and the
(Yog Sothoth)

and the
(hatred already bone
marrow already)

(and the
hatred)

o end
o thousand–year–old butterfly

➤ 30

cáncer enmarañada primavera
(día de abajo)   no preguntes
por un hueco de pájaros
por una sílaba de pan

➤   30

cancer entangled spring
(day from below)   don't ask
for a crevice of birds
for a syllable of bread

aborto de poema en oficina pública

ya   ya
u   no   u
mano   umano
por aquí
primera puerta
a la derecha por favor
tire empuje
no está se fue no
tan a la derecha por favooorr
o se equivocará de   VOOORR
sucar   neoliva
¿sí? tanle   jos   que *¿sí por favor?*
su   car   ne*allá doblando la escalera*
¿sí? tarde   ya   yago *no se encuentra*
¿ve?no está   quería
sumitad   infier *vuelva mañana* no
más   u   no   ya
¿sí?
NADAH

➤ 31

abortion of poem in a public office

soon   soon
u   no   u
man   uman
this way
first door
to the right please
pull push
not here left not
so much to the right pleease
or you take the wrong   EEASE
hisfle   sholive
*yes?*sof   ar   that *yesplease?*
his   fle   sh*overthere round the st*air
yes?   late   soon   soon *not here*
see?not here   i wanted
hishalf   infer *come back tomorrow* no
plus   u   no   soon
yes?
NOHTHING

➤   32

nacimiento II

vomitar sueños
croar de pena   de lejanía
llevar alimento a una torre

abrir dos ojos a la vez
aunque la cuerda salte
y algo llore en la noche del ropero

birth II

to vomit dreams
to croak out of pain   out of distance
to take food to a tower

to open two eyes at once
even if the spring breaks
and something cries in the night of the wardrobe

aquella amiga desesperación
y es posible todavía
soñar un pantano con cara de niño

rodeada de bienes
se derrumba esta casa

fantasmas de destinos
que se aparecen   a los que sigue
un pájaro de sol   con un dardo de aire en las venas
un muro de rumor
apedreado por la suerte
figuras de un lado solo   y matan

➢   33

that friend–despair
and it is still possible
to dream a swamp with a child's face

surrounded by possessions
this house collapses

ghosts of destinies
that appear   followed by
a bird of sun   dart of air in its veins
a wall of whispers
stoned by fate
figures on one side only   and they kill

abres   sí   túnel
de claridá rabiosa   entretienes
al ser del sueño

no es el camino es la flecha
equivocada
el animal sangrante y
futuro

➤   34

you open   yes   tunnel
of violent clarity   you entertain
the creature of dream

it is not the road it's the wrong
arrow
the animal bleeding and
to come

condenados a un signo
a un vestido sin brazos
también los caminos se niegan
nombres de algo extinguido afloran
formas de nada se adhieren a la que huye
nosotros   nuestras algas
   de humo
en el morirse ejecutado minucioso
quizá de una bebida
para siempre ante aquella boca

y en el cielo de quebrarse y en el cielo de arder
su oscuridad perdida
en ropas de nieve canta

condemned to a sign
to a dress without arms
even the roads say no
names of something dead surface
shapes of nothing cling to her who runs away
we   our seaweeds
    of smoke
in the perpetrated death meticulous
perhaps of a drink
forever before that mouth

and in the breaking sky in the burning sky
her lost darkness
in clothes of snow sings

alcanzo esa mano esa pura música
deshecha entre nombres que sostienen
solo algo pardo   algo podrido
alimento para ojos que no abandonan la casa
la torre imposible de los huesos
contra todo invasor   esa pura música
muerde el adiós   llora en qué luces la retienen

i reach that hand that pure music
undone among names which hold
only something brown   something rotten
food for eyes that do not leave the house
the impossible tower of the bones
against all invaders   that pure music
bites the good–bye   cries what lights they hold her under

un mal se apaga solo si otro mal crece
una lluvia seca hiere el sol   la memoria
no alcanza   entre dormidas piernas
un silencio con bosque   al tiro ciego
lo festeja sin ira la oca de nube
un mal se apaga   dice apenas
este nombre   una flor de vacío
solo si otro mal crece

solo si otro mal crece
y el hambre olvida y canta
en la noche de su guerra
en el desnudo y fin de su guerra
en el sur y salvaje y caminaré de su guerra

an evil dies only if another evil grows
a dry rain wounds the sun   memory
does not reach   among sleeping legs
a silence with woods   the goose cloud
celebrates the blind shot without anger
an evil dies   a flower of emptiness
barely says   this name
only if another evil grows

only if another evil grows
and hunger forgets and sings
in the night of its war
in the naked and end of its war
in the south and wild and i will walk of its war

y las palabras

y las
palabras

y los patios   que arderán
mucho después del sol
ya atravesados por ningún mal   pasos
ningunos abrazados

y los patios   y las palabras

and the words

and the
words

and the patios   that burn
long after the sun
no longer crossed by any evil   no
steps embraced

and the patios   and the words

la rueda se ha detenido   se ha deteni-
dos tres dos tres dos   la rueda
se ha detenido   roto por dentro
solo madera   entran ojos
solo memoria   cónico
solo memoria   al cielo de cara no es posible
que arda ya más que arda más todavía   que
arda sola eterna como si el viento   (algo)
no arrojara sus migas sus ropas   deshecho
ansiado cuerpo luz de la noche   pájaros
homicidas bajo el puente   se alejan fríos
(algo) cadenciosos   mar
y silbó y dijo   criatura barro
y dijo y rió   trompa de vena
y rió apuntó   carne temblada
y disparó   bulto
          zapatos
          carne
aéreo   (algo)
y sol   (una mujer)
hachas de sol   (ante la puerta con llave)
arañan la puerta   (busca su llave) aclara

the wheel has stopped   stop–
two three two three two   the wheel
has stopped   broken inside
only wood   eyes enter
only memory   conic
only memory   face to the sky it is not possible
that she should still burn more should burn still more
burn alone eternal as if the wind   (something)
would not scatter her crumbs her clothes   undone
desired body light of the night   birds
homicides under the bridge   go away cold
(something) in cadence   sea
and it whistled and said   creature mud
said and laughed   trumpet of vein
laughed aimed   trembled flesh
and fired   bundle
          shoes
          flesh
ethereal   (something)
and sun   (a woman)
hatchets of sun   (before the locked door)
scratch the door   (looks for her key) it clears

el pecho (dice en alta voz) el ojo (ábreme yo) la
                                        [mano
(llama llama) el borde (no) del río (no) de sangre
(no) de sangre que huye hilo salvaje negro de pavor
entre el suelo y la puerta al encuentro de sus pasos
la rueda se ha detenido   se ha deteni-
dos tres dos tres dos   la rueda
se ha detenido

her chest (says in a loud voice) her eye (open to me i) her
                                                     [hand
(calls calls) the edge (no) of the river (no) of blood
(no) of blood that runs away wild thread black with fear
between threshold and door meeting her steps
the wheel has stopped   stop–
two three two three two   the wheel
has stopped

EPILOGUE

On February 17, 1968, when Susana Thénon was beginning to write the first poems of this collection, she wrote to me:

> In this letter I am sending you two poems of the "new" series, the only ones so far that I consider finished. The series is called *distancias*, though I cannot explain clearly why. I only know that these poems are related to alienation, to loneliness, to the tragic and gentle perishability of language, to the "distance", even if minimal, that exists between us and ourselves, or between us and the other.

Thus, since 1968, I have witnessed the growth of a unique textual experience, interrupted by long silences (1970–1982) which she devoted to photography. In this field too Susana Thénon displays a masterly command of language. Then, she resumed and reorganized her work and the result is the book she offers us now. I can call *distances* a unique textual experience because of the complexity of the simultaneous relationships Susana Thénon establishes in all directions and at all levels: a moving net within each poem as well as within the succession of poems, always in flux.

Taken together, these poems create a space which, paradoxically, opens with vanishing lines and simultaneously closes with anguishing circularity. Susana Thénon fragments, breaks up, tears up and, at the same time, organizes a poetical constellation which then reveals itself to the reader through its pure presence. This is both surprising and inevitable. Its strangeness does not prevent communication. On the contrary, it begs for it, spurs it. Through the many voices that carry on the dialogue, the book tells the reader, "Search. I'm multiple. Don't stop. Don't be satisfied."

In the work of Susana Thénon, spatial imagination bears special significance. It is enough to remember the titles of her previous works: *Aledaños/Boundaries*, one section of *Edad sin tregua/Age without Rest* (1958), *Habitante de la nada/Inhabitant of Nothingness* (1959), *de lugares extraños/from strange places* (1967), to which now she adds *distancias/distances*. Boundaries, strange places, ambits that are real, concrete, precise to the point of pain, or that transform themselves into dream, into memory, into the longed-for and never reachable heaven, into nothingness. In *distances* these spaces acquire a quality which I could only define by repeating the words of Antonin Artaud in *Le Pèse-nerfs*:

Nous sommes quelques-uns à cette époque à avoir voulu attenter aux choses, créer en nous des espaces à la vie, des espaces qui n'étaient pas et ne semblaient pas devoir trouver place dans l'espace.

[There are a few of us at this time who have wanted to make an attempt against things, to create within ourselves spaces toward life, spaces that did not exist and did not seem able to find a place in space.–R.T.]

With intensity and lucidity, *distances* attests to the search "without rest" for this impossible space. Name of ambits that are never heaven, or the center, or plenitude, or paradise, are scattered throughout *distances*. There is the eternal wandering around the outskirts of the world, never perceiving *the* place (not even *a* place).

The poetical voice simply attests to its condition of being in exile, of never having known its native land, the one to which it might have truly belonged. Here is born the particular quality of its "time" and "memory", divested of past, of hope, of future. "Spaces that did not seem able to find a place in space," as Artaud wanted; times without time as it happens in the alternating voices of that memorable *distance* #4: "there's a country/ (but not mine) / where night is only in the afternoon / (but not ours)". Or, in *distance* #17: "how long time takes / (those woods) / grief to grieve that does not let / (wind woods)", where one lives in a void without time, remembering a past ("those woods") and yearning for that other past that will come again from the future (perhaps in the manner of Saint Paul–Borges, with a memory that will come to us from the future).

However, a page from *distances* will surprise us unexpectedly with the coexistence of hope, humor, or a longing for the dream together with horror of life, of blind fate, of the limit of madness; but, above all, with the unexpected appearance of tenderness in that empty and tight-locked inferno. A dream "where terror and music talk to each other again" (#8), that "gentle stuff alive / on sick earth" (#7) and the "moon like ancient music / one catches alive / in the gardens of the Social Club" (#19), where humor mingles with tenderness; in those dark zones where the "flower" comes up (#7 or #14), but especially in #24 where the poem struggles to build an "airy country". Stubborn parentheses pierce the body of the text (Artaud's spaces) where "(one morning)", "(and its fire-works")", "(and its flower)" insist till they break the text and open it in the final line, without any graphic barriers to trap it in: "against the impending fear (the impossible) / already (and its flower". From time to time, humor also eases up the packed-to-bursting chain of poems. It is enough to remember the humor that permeates the poem "annunciation" (#16) where a crevice opens ("ancient *Landschaft* opening on Ghent"). This crevice is as soothing as the background visible in a Flemish painting.

A contradictory language reads and translates a contradictory world fraught with simultaneous opposites, with metamorphic processes, with sudden breaks and recompositions. The largest wealth of relationships combines with the starkest nakedness, extreme discipline watches over chaos.

Metamorphoses and self-metamorphoses occur at the imaginary and at the individual levels, ("and i with myself (and always) with love unmoved") (#4). There is metamorphosis of a place that unfolds and folds back on itself ("there breathes in / the park / place above itself") (#22), of night which says in a dead language "*i am two / one equals one / without forever*" (#17). These metamorphoses seem to culminate in that vortex of transformations which is *distance* #13, where the poetic voice – the night's – falls abruptly from on high in vertiginous chain toward its end: "bitter accomplice / of the dayless awakening / i feed on eyelid shine of dead lark".

At the level of language, the writing accomplishes a parallel activity: the plural becomes singular ("tus árbol / your tree") (#18) [TRANSLATOR'S NOTE: this is one example of what cannot be translated into English since in English adjectives lack gender and number.]; the phonic significant loses its consonants in order to make the word lighter in keeping with its meaning and then recomposes in its original form ("volar   oar   volar / to fly   igh to fly") (#18). [TRANSLATOR'S NOTE: this translator was able to achieve a similar effect by dropping the consonants and spell the remaining vowel–sounds in such a way that they would convey no other meaning except an echo–like effect.]; nouns become adjectives and combine with other nouns to revert afterwards to their play of central and marginal categories ("i read / your wolf– laughter white language") #6.

Contradictions fill Susana Thénon's space in manifestations that are simultaneous or in process and which range from duality (plurality) to unity and viceversa. In this regard, one should mention the hermaphrodite which, Susana Thénon admits, she sees not only as a myth but also as a prophecy beyond any ethical or philosophical consideration. One can see it in #19 ("he laughed that is   i"), but it also surfaces indirectly and insistently in the feminine and masculine voices of the utterance and in her special handling of language.

I refer to poems #1 and #39 which open and close the collection and which intensify the syntactical–semantic net of relationships between contiguous or distant elements. These links are often unclear because of the placement–pattern (a word, or a line depending on its construction, may combine with a word or a line far away, and this may occur either before or after, inside or outside the parentheses, in connections resulting from a vertical or linear reading) and because of the grammatical–patterns (an element may be both subject of a verb and object of another.) All this is aggravated by the ambiguity of the morphology. Indeed, this relates explicitly, I believe, to a linguistic manifestation of hermaphrodism built into the Spanish language. Our nouns belong to either the masculine or the feminine gender. Gender in Spanish is repeated and reinforced by the adjective ending [–o(s) / –a(s)]. The ending –o may also refer to a neutral pronoun form (i.e.

algo / something). But, at the same time, noun gender may or may not refer to natural gender, that is, to the sex of what is named (gender and sex coincide in *el mono / the monkey* or *la ladrona / the female thief*, but not in *la rueda* (f.) */ the wheel* or *el martillo* (m.) */ the hammer*). The problem is compounded by lack of coincidences which the context may or may not make clear, i.e. *creatura / creature* (f. and/or m.) or *barro / clay* (m.), where *creatura* is grammatically feminine but the word may be used for either sex.

distance #1, among other poems, confronts the reader with unclear situations which require answers: "a woman" (why not many?): "broken inside", "conic" (who?); "undone" ("the wind?" "something?" the "desired body"?). It confronts us also with words in isolation, words of absolute value, hard and crushing signs which resist all connections and which entrench themselves in the blank spaces that surround them (i.e. "conic" in the fifth line, or "sea" in the twelfth).

The working of the poem in its distribution on the page, the fractures, the blanks that function like silences in a musical score, the parentheses and the italics which translate the alternating voices are indispensable games. They are the exact formulation, the exact "naming." The dialogues the poetical voices engage in (reminding us of the plural voices and the freedom of contemporary music) are internal dialogues of the text which somehow adumbrate the multiplicity of the external infinite dialogue of *distancias/distances* with the reader.

Thus, Susana Thénon has been able to say that her reader, "architect of her/his own text, may in turn build [it] and tear [it] down", and she has been able to wish "that the reader may become a poem, another poem, almost skipping the stage of creation, becoming directly the thing created."

Ana María Barrenechea
December 1983 – January 1984
Translated by Renata Treitel

TRANSLATOR'S AFTERWORD

In an illuminating article on the problems of fidelity and betrayal in translation, Paul Mann states that fidelity to source means that "translation is difference."[1] Though this statement may sound paradoxical, he reminds us that translation is writing, and writing contains an internalized absence (or ambiguity, or difference) which is the distance that occurs any time speech is committed to paper, thus becoming writing. In other words, writing renders speech "always already absent." This concept has its origin in Saussure. Internalized absence (or ambiguity, or difference) is inherent to any kind of writing and it establishes the open space in any text in which meaning takes place. This space is what concerns Derrida and the deconstructionists: they explore that open space (which they call "dynamic space") because it is there that meaning occurs. In other words, a reader has to explore the "dynamic space" in order to understand how a text comes to mean. However, by its very nature (ambiguity) this space reveals a dynamic process that points to the "instability" of the text. Therefore, a text cannot be reduced to monological meaning.

A translator, like any other reader, is faced with a text that generates a multiplicity of meanings. Therefore, her task is to discover, reveal, and preserve the dynamic process of the original. However, her task is complicated by the fact that, to the above-mentioned dynamic process, she adds the dynamic process posed by the distance that exists between the original text and the translation. The goal of a good translation is to transfer those dynamic spaces and make room, in turn, for as much ambiguity as it exists in the original. In other words, a translation should "be as difficult as its source."

Given the above, the difficulty of translating *distancias* becomes apparent when one considers that Susana Thénon compounds the natural problems of translation by submitting both language and poetical form to unbelievable deformations. However, it is precisely through these deformations (or excesses, or transgressions) that "new meanings come to be."[2] In the measure that the

[111]

translator understands them and preserves them can the reader share in Susana Thénon's world.

Perhaps a short description of the difficulties of Susana Thénon's language is in order at this point, but I will limit my discussion to the problems of her language as they affect the act of translation.

With a few exceptions, Susana Thénon's diction is simple. Yet the reader is constantly brought to a stop by the realization that he/she understands the words but not their meaning. At best, *distancias* offers the reader only a slippery terrain. Even the simplest words seem to point in different directions. If the reader is conscientious, he/she begins to question every word for its grammatical function and for its real meaning because, wrenched out of ordinary context–the language in *distancias* being deformed–words can be construed in different ways. Indeed, to translate Susana Thénon is to discover how tenuous the web that holds language together is. Deprived of connections, or in total isolation or placed in incongruous positions, words recover their freedom and stop communicating. Or, juxtaposed in unexpected grammatical ways, words suddenly say too much.

As I worked on *distancias,* I realized that Susana Thénon required a literal translation even to the point of choosing words which might be construed in their double (or triple) grammatical function if this feature was present in the original. However, the criterion of literality would become an obstacle whenever I had to choose between two different meanings of an ambiguous word or expression: i.e., *"a secas"* (#15, line 2) might mean "plainly" and refer to the whole utterance ("plainly or in plain words") or "dry" referring to lack of alcoholic beverages because "there were no taverns left." The second meaning was chosen after consulting with the author. Or, when the context did not provide the necessary clues: i.e., *"sueño"* (#20, line 7), since it is not clear from the context whether it should be translated as "sleep" or as "dream." Again, the author was consulted. In such cases, literality was abandoned and the English was brought closer to the intended meaning even if this carried the implicit danger of increasing the degree of elucidation: i.e., *"tus letras"* #20, line 8) refers to the alphabet. In English, the word "letters" may mean either the letters of the alphabet or any form of written communication. The new construction was chosen in order to avoid the unwarranted ambiguity in English. Or *"manos"* (#13, line 10), the article was introduced before the word "hands" to prevent the verbal sequence "ejects fires" from casting a verbal connotation on the English noun "hands."

Decisions of this kind were not taken lightly and changes were made only after many discussions with the author. However, the rule of literality was adhered to for most of the manuscript and any departure from it was out of necessity and after much thought. In the following paragraphs, I will try to give a few examples of the problems I encountered and how I solved them and why.

In #1, lines 1 and 2, *"la rueda se ha detenido   se ha deteni / dos tres dos tres dos"* ("the wheel has stopped   stop/two"), Ms. Thénon changes *"detenido"* into *"detenidos."* This plural triggers off all sorts of implications and complications. *"Deteni/dos"* suddenly does not refer to *"la rueda"* ("the wheel") anymore or, if it does, it also refers to something or somebody else (*¿estamos detenidos? ¿están detenidos?*). But then, what is the new subject? The poem does not provide an answer. Another problem is caused by the way Ms. Thénon breaks the word *"deteni/dos"*: here the eye moves to the next line expecting fulfillment in the repetition of *"detenido."* But suddenly the last syllable undergoes a transformation, loses its link with *detener* (to stop) and goes off on its own to become the beginning of the numerical sequence *"dos tres dos tres dos."* Unfortunately the English language does not make room for these variations so that all but one of the above implications are irremediably lost and the numerical sequence is salvaged only because the stopped sound of the past tense ending blends in with the initial /t/ of the word "two."

In #18, line 2, Ms. Thénon writes *"lube sobre agua"* ("cloon on water.") Neither *"lube"* nor "cloon" exist in the dictionaries. The author coins a new word which incorporates some elements from *luna* (moon) and *nube* (cloud). In translating this word, it was important to preserve the long vowel sound /oo/ of *luna* which the word moon conveniently provided and the liquid sound of /

[113]

l/ which, by accident, is present in the cluster /cl/ of cloud. By using these two sounds at the beginning of the translated word, I felt I was coming very close to the original. The rest followed.

Susana Thénon coins a new verb in #9, line 9, *"el viento hidraba"* ("the hydra-wind was howling"). *Hidrar* is not a Spanish word. However, it evokes perfectly the image of water and that of the mythical Hydra, the many-headed snake of Lerna. The juxtaposition of *"viento"* and *hidrar* conveys with economy of means the fury of the wind as it pushes the waters up in such a way that wind and water become almost one. Rather than coining a new word in the manner of Susana Thénon, i.e., "to hydre," I preferred to transfer the excess of her verbal form to the noun, hence "the hydra-wind," and reinforce the meaning with the verb "to howl."

Some of Ms. Thénon's transgressions in *distancias* are games, word games, but they serve a purpose. For instance, a word breaks and the pieces recompose on the same line (horizontal reading) or on this line and the following one (vertical reading). Take #31, lines 2 and 3:

u   no   u

mano   u   mano

The first transgression is in the spelling. Like in English, *humano* in Spanish is spelled with an /h/. However, given the Spanish phonetical system, Susana Thénon's transgression becomes apparent only to the eye that reads. One might well wonder why the author introduces this transgression. My explanation is that she uses this device to lessen the image of man/woman, which is already quite diminished at this point of *distancias*. In fact, in *distancias,* man/woman is depicted in its purest form, i.e., #1, #7, #9, #12, etc. But, man/woman's essence gets tarnished the longer he/she is in touch with the "real" world (which in *distancias* it is the "unreal" one). By making man/woman *"umano"* (note the masculine!) rather than *"humano,"* Ms. Thénon makes the word converge to the meaning implied in #31. Not content with this, she breaks the word up and plays with the fragments *"u," "no," "mano,"* which by themselves or together range from no meaning (*"u,"*) to

[114]

negation ("*no*") to synecdoche ("*mano*"). Then she recombines them in "*umano*" both in the vertical reading of lines 2 and 3 or in the linear (horizontal) reading of line 2. But whereas she pretends to show man/woman as emptied of his/her humanness, what she is really doing is to reiterate no-meaning. The word has been emptied of meaning. It has become an empty sign. This game was impossible to duplicate in English. After many attempts, the version

u   no   u

man   uman

was chosen because of its obvious advantages over other possibilities. For instance, "u", meaningless in itself, reads like "you" so that the suggestion of "*uno*" (one or someone) is preserved; the negation (very important in all of *distancias*) survives and the juxtaposition of "u" (you) and "no" negates the possibility that somebody might really exist. It also preserves for the English-speaking reader the connotation of "one," because so many words in English have the prefix "uni–" (i.e., unison). The word "man" rather than "hand" was introduced to keep the game alive. And "man" may be a synecdoche of human. The same word game is repeated in the vertical reading of lines 16 and 17: "*su mitad más uno*" ("his half plus u(you) no"). As it happened above, the word "no" negates what has been said.

It was not possible to translate another word game of #31. The word "*ya*" ("soon") which the poet stammers in the public office undergoes a sudden transformation: instead of moving smoothly from "*ya*" to "*no*" (line 14), this negation interferes with "*ya*" and the poet makes a mental association which comes out as "*yago*" (Yago/Iago) from Othello. The voice of the employee picks up the negation and the dialogue (if we can call it such) comes to a climactic end in the word "*NADAH*" ("NOHTHING"), Susana Thénon's triumphant final transgression.

Some of the word games play on the vowel sounds. For example, in #17, line 3, the author establishes the sequence "*dolor doler*" ("grief to grieve") where the progression from noun to verb

[115]

is given by the phoneme /e/. It was not possible to duplicate this in translation, but the similarity between "grief" and "to grieve" carries the echo-like quality of the Spanish line.

A more difficult problem occurs in #10, lines 7, 8 and 9: *"porque sí porque sí/nunca por ¿ah?/por ¿ih?"* ("because because / never for ah?/ for auh?"). The expression *"¿ah?"* has the value of an exclamation and as such it was translated. However, *"¿ih?"* ("auh?") echoes the vowel sound of the word *"sí"* which was not translated literally. The closest thing to do was to play on the stressed syllable of "because." The echo-like quality is preserved and so is the mocking attitude.

Where Susana Thénon juxtaposes two nouns giving one of them an adjectival function, a compound form was used because of its compatibility with the English language (i.e., #5, line 10; #6, line 11, #13, line 7). Finally, when the English line does not correspond to the Spanish line, the disruption was produced by the needs of the English syntax (i.e., #9, lines 11 and 12; #18, lines 8 and 9, etc.)

To translate Susana Thénon has been to live in a state of discovery. On hindsight, *distancias* appears far more accessible than at the beginning of the translation because the transgressions, which make the book difficult, become inseparable from meaning. They become the vehicle through which we experience Susana Thénon's vision of the world. "I must represent chaos with chaos." So she creates a chaotic form, but form nonetheless. Reality and language suffer loss of cohesion. Likewise, the shape (form) of the poem is broken and the elements are scattered across the blank page so that the poem incorporates space as one more formal element. Freed from conventional imperatives, the dimensions of the work multiply and so do the possibilities of interpretation. The work has become polymorphous and it communicates in the measure that the reader is willing to share in the act of discovery.

Renata Treitel
January 1984

1   "Translation and Literary Criticism: A Response to Rainer Schulte," *Translation Review*, 13 (1983): 8–17.

2   Grass, Vernon W., ed., *European Literary Theory and Practice: From Existential Phenomenology to Structuralism* (New York: Dell Publishing Co., 1973) 7.

SUSANA THÉNON

Born in 1937, Argentine poet Susana Thénon was also a translator and artistic photographer. Her collections of published poetry include *Edad sin tregua* (1958), *Habitante de la nada* (1960), *de lugares extraños* (1967), *distancias* (1984), and *Ova completa* (1987). Among her unpublished work at the time of her death in 1990 are *Ensayo general* and *papyrus*. Thénon's work has been translated in many European and American literary journals.

The translator, Renata Treitel, was educated in Italy, Argentina, and the United States. She has published one collection of poetry, *German Notebook*, and has published translations in numerous journals. She currently teaches Spanish and Italian at Tulsa Junior College. In 1991 she won the Witter Bynner Translation Award for her translation of Rosita Copioli's *Splendida Lumina Solis*, which will be published by Sun & Moon Press in 1994.

SUN & MOON CLASSICS

The Sun & Moon Classics is a publicly supported, nonprofit program to publish new editions, translations, or republications of outstanding world literature of the late nineteenth and twentieth centuries. Through its publication of living authors as well as great masters of the century, the series attempts to redefine what usually is meant by the idea of a "classic" by dehistoricizing the concept and embracing a new, ever changing literary canon.

Organized by the Contemporary Arts Educational Project, Inc., a nonprofit corporation, and published by its program Sun & Moon Press, the series is made possible, in part, by grants and individual contributions.

This book was made possible, in part, through matching grants from the National Endowment for the Arts and from the California Arts Council, through an organizational grant from the Andrew W. Mellon Foundation, through a grant for advertising and promotion from the Lila B. Wallace/ Reader's Digest Fund, and through contributions from the following individuals:

Charles Altieri (Seattle, Washington)
John Arden (Galway, Ireland)
Jesse Huntley Ausubel (New York, New York)
Dennis Barone (West Hartford, Connecticut)
Jonathan Baumbach (Brooklyn, New York)
Guy Bennett (Los Angeles, California)
Bill Berkson (Bolinas, California)
Steve Benson (Berkeley, California)
Charles Bernstein and Susan Bee (New York, New York)
Sherry Bernstein (New York, New York)
Dorothy Bilik (Silver Spring, Maryland)
Bill Corbett (Boston, Massachusetts)
Fielding Dawson (New York, New York)
Robert Crosson (Los Angeles, California)
Tina Darragh and P. Inman (Greenbelt, Maryland)
David Detrich (Los Angeles, California)
Christopher Dewdney (Toronto, Canada)
Philip Dunne (Malibu, California)
George Economou (Norman, Oklahoma)
Elaine Equi and Jerome Sala (New York, New York)
Lawrence Ferlinghetti (San Francisco, California)
Richard Foreman (New York, New York)

Howard N. Fox (Los Angeles, California)
Jerry Fox (Aventura, Florida)
In Memoriam: Rose Fox
Melvyn Freilicher (San Diego, California)
Miro Gavran (Zagreb, Croatia)
Peter Glassgold (Brooklyn, New York)
Barbara Guest (New York, New York)
Perla and Amiram V. Karney (Bel Air, California)
Fred Haines (Los Angeles, California)
Fanny Howe (La Jolla, California)
Harold Jaffe (San Diego, California)
Ira S. Jaffe (Albuquerque, New Mexico)
Alex Katz (New York, New York)
Tom LaFarge (New York, New York)
Mary Jane Lafferty (Los Angeles, California)
Michael Lally (Santa Monica, California)
Norman Lavers (Jonesboro, Arkansas)
Jerome Lawrence (Malibu, California)
Stacey Levine (Seattle, Washington)
Herbert Lust (Greenwich, Connecticut)
Norman MacAffee (New York, New York)
Rosemary Macchiavelli (Washington, DC)
Beatrice Manley (Los Angeles, California)
Martin Nakell (Los Angeles, California)
Toby Olson (Philadelphia, Pennsylvania)
Maggie O'Sullivan (Hebden Bridge, England)
Rochelle Owens (Norman, Oklahoma)
Marjorie and Joseph Perloff (Pacific Palisades, California)
Dennis Phillips (Los Angeles, California)
David Reed (New York, New York)
Ishmael Reed (Oakland, California)
Janet Rodney (Santa Fe, New Mexico)
Joe Ross (Washington, DC)
Dr. Marvin and Ruth Sackner (Miami Beach, Florida)
Floyd Salas (Berkeley, California)
Tom Savage (New York, New York)
Leslie Scalapino (Oakland, California)
James Sherry (New York, New York)
Aaron Shurin (San Francisco, California)
Charles Simic (Strafford, New Hampshire)
Gilbert Sorrentino (Stanford, California)

Catharine R. Stimpson (Staten Island, New York)
John Taggart (Newburg, Pennsylvania)
Nathaniel Tarn (Tesuque, New Mexico)
Fiona Templeton (New York, New York)
Mitch Tuchman (Los Angeles, California)
Wendy Walker (New York, New York)
Anne Walter (Carnac, France)
Arnold Wesker (Hay on Wye, England)

If you would like to be a contributor to this series, please send your tax-deductible contribution to The Contemporary Arts Educational Project, Inc., a non-profit corporation, 6026 Wilshire Boulevard, Los Angeles, California 90036.

BOOKS IN THE SUN & MOON CLASSICS

*First American publication
**Revised edition